DARKNESS AND LIGHTNESS

Observations, moments of dark and light we all experience in life

Norman Rivera Gonzalez

Blog
nrgwriting.com/blog/

Copyright © Norman Rivera Gonzalez

ISBN 978-0-9979813-0-8

All rights reserved. This book or any portion thereof
may not be reproduced or used in any manner whatsoever
without the express written permission of the publisher
except for the use of brief quotations in a book review.

Inquiries & Contact Information:

nrgwriting@gmail.com

Facebook: NRG Writing

Twitter: @nrgwriting

TABLE OF CONTENTS

	Page
Foreword	1
Acknowledgements	4
Introduction	7

Chapters

1-	Gilded Cage	11
2-	Red Choo Choo Train	15
3-	Dark Cocoon	20
4-	Second Chance At Living	22
5-	Fleeting Anger	27
6-	Gratefulness	30
7-	Darkness Descends	32
8-	Hi Daddy	35
9-	Deep Darkness Of Sleep	39
10-	My Wish	42
11-	Scream	45

12-	The Healing Of The Divine	47
13-	The Unwelcome Visitor	51
14-	Thank You	55
15-	Unsustainable Anger	57
16-	The Light House	60
17-	The Year 2016	64
18-	Sandman's Visit	67
19-	Remember	70
20-	Beloved Ancestors	75
21-	Accepting Accountability	78
22-	Ask And Ye Shall Receive	85
23-	Hear My Plea	88
24-	Like That Man	91
25-	I Forgive You	95
26-	The Unspoken Of Sanctuary	98
27-	Sense Of Hopelessness	101

28-	How Are You?	104
29-	Reality Or Imagination	108
30-	Divine Saint Michael	111
31-	Breaking Free From The Dark Web	114
32-	Is The Light Real?	108
33-	My Sweet Jesus	120
34-	Life	122
35-	Grant Me Peace	126
36-	Beloved Guardian Angels	129
37-	The Rooster's Song	131
38-	Encased By White Debris	134

FOREWORD

Victor Pagán

Depression with its feelings of sadness, tearfulness, emptiness, and at times helplessness affects millions of people throughout the world. In his book "Darkness and Lightness" Mr. Rivera Gonzalez has put the feelings he has experiencing into words. In doing so, he could examine what he had written at a later date and share that experience with his friends and therapist. His words allowed me to understand what he was going through much better.

He has waged a war against depression and anxiety and the weapon he is using is the written word. In reading his work you begin to sense a pattern. One dark moment followed by a lighter moment. Like waves on an ocean. Depression usually occurs in that manner, one good day followed by a darker, deeper episode. The fact that he has been able to document his episodes and commit them to writing is an indication that he is winning the battle

I highly recommend this book to those who are engaged in the same struggles as Mr. Rivera Gonzalez and have not discovered a venue to use against their battle with depression and anxiety. In reading these notes they will discover that they are not alone.

Victor Pagán, RN, MPH

ACKNOWLEDGMENTS

I owe so much gratitude to all who encouraged and supported me to write this book.

Some of the names I mention below are only a few of many that pushed me on.

My loving Mother Palmira Gonzalez Nuncy, her support has been nourishing and helpful in so many ways in my goal to healing.

Joseph (Joe) Bonanno, Victor Pagan, faithful friends (perhaps brothers from another lifetime) that have inspired me to allow my writing to be read by the world.

My strong friend Thomas Wirth who insisted I get professional mental health to deal with my issues.

My sincere thank you to Dr. Roger V. Davenport and Dr. Tatiana Nagornaia (Brooklyn, NYC) for your words of wisdom and invaluable therapy.

All my friends that enjoyed my writing and could relate to my mental condition.

Rosemary Grillo. Upon running into you during a winter day, you touched me with the words "You're not alone". I will never forget that encounter.

Rose Rivera. Thank you for your vision and help in compiling my writing and your technological skills. Your friendship will always be appreciated.

Friends that enjoyed my writing and told me to publish and share with the universe.

There are no words that can describe the gratitude I have for God (in all your manifestations). God, my ancestors, spiritual guides and Orishas have been my anchors during the dark times. You are that light at the end of the tunnel.

There are so many more that have been supportive and lent their shoulder for me to lean on and your graciousness will never be forgotten.

May my personal journey enlighten and bring peace to yours.

INTRODUCTION

"You are not alone."

Those were the meaningful words that my friend Rosemary told me as we say good bye to each other on a cold winter day outside on the sidewalk.

It was an "aha" moment, which meant so much to me.

We hadn't seen each other in a couple of years, it was a quick significant conversation.

I confided my condition battling depression and anxiety. She shared hers and the tools she used to manage it. I had no idea she was facing the same challenges and appreciated her sharing her experience.

We listened to each other.

A short conversation and very heartfelt.

We hugged each other and said good bye.

I am not alone.

I have a great support system that has helped me through these difficult times. Friends, family and professional help.

Writing has been a most helpful tool for me.

What I share with you in this book are my most personal intimate moments of highs and lows in my battle.

There were very dark abysmal moments, yet; hope, spirituality and light lifted me at the appropriate time.

It was great timing.

I was not alone.

Initially, I kept the writing to myself.

It was very personal.

Then I decided, what the heck, share with friends and loved ones so that I could be better understood.

They were appreciative that I shared my innermost intimate thoughts and they were able to comprehend my state of mind.

They enjoyed my writing, both dark and light. At times, concerned, but knew I was on the right track.

Many of them were able to relate and say, "You channeled my thoughts and feelings".

I was not alone.

Hence, I'm not a closet writer any longer.

My sincere desire as I share my writing, is that it is inspirational and healing to you.

You will notice as you read my thoughts, that at the end, my glass is half full.

"You are not alone."

Gilded Cage

Trapped.

Living in this gilded cage provides a false sense of comfort.

All that seems necessary to survive and feel secure, it is not enough.

But I may be telling a little white lie to myself, I do feel some comfort.

A sense of security, of safety.

Seeds for nutrition and fresh water is available frequently to allow me to live.

The inside of my cage are decorated with plants that do not have a scent, do not appear to be alive.

These plants are clever imitations of the real ones.

A false sense of reality.

A small mirror has been attached to one of the walls of the cage, which I can reach from my perch.

The mirror allowing me to see a glimpse of who I am, in the background, of where I am.

The mirror reveals my face and expansive wings.

Although not entirely visible, I notice that some feathers on my wings are damaged, somehow clipped and ugly.

I ruffle my feathers to see if this action allows them to appear natural, normal.

It does not.

I carefully groom my wings with my beak, to cover, camouflage the damage.

Yes, giving the appearance of normality, hoping no one notices the flaws.

Many times, the cage door is open, where I can sit and see the four walls that surround my gilded cage.

From here I focus, and hear familiar sounds coming from outside the four walls.

I would love to see the faces of the creatures associated with those sounds.

I wish to jump and fly off of the opened cage door to experience the outside.

Yet, as much as I try, my wings are damaged.

I cannot fly.

Although difficult to perceive such a thing, I know instinctively, that eventually the damaged feathers will heal.

I will be able to fly and soar around the room.

Hopefully, the windows within the room will be open, where I can fly out freely without looking back.

Then, I will fly and soar as high as I can.

I will be amongst the natural environment where I am meant to be.

I only hope and pray, that the valor to fly will be present.

Red Choo Choo Train

The fire engine red Choo Choo Train has traveled thousands of miles.

Through all types of weather and railroad conditions.

The fiery sun, the cold snow.

The comforting shade.

The intact railroad tracks.

The railroad tracks that are barely up to par.

Carrying passengers both old and young to their destinations.

At times, the cars full to capacity with people of all backgrounds.

Other times, passengers barely onboard.

Still, with or without passengers, the train goes full steam ahead and stopped at all scheduled destinations.

Through the thousands of miles, this train has been weathered.

The brilliant red on some of the train cars have faded.

Some of the paint has been chipped.

The train is viewed by a variety of eyes.

Some see it as a formidable, strong and still brilliant functioning train.

Others may see it as a train that should be hidden in car train graveyards.

Perhaps not fond of the strong foundation of trains and what they represent.

Those that see it in the latter, may not see the potential of this train.

That could be for a variety of reasons.

Perhaps unhappy or bitterness has set into their lives.

Perhaps their view is through a glass half empty.

This is a train that has derailed during its existence, yet, professional dedicated engineers were able to bring it back on track.

Back to its fiery glory and many rejoice to see it running forward on the railroad tracks.

It's a beautiful special train.

A train that brings joy to children and adults alike as it races by their neighborhoods.

Children chasing the glorious train with joy in their hearts and smiles on their faces.

There have been moments where it almost derailed again, but held steadfast and kept running.

The unhappy ones, wishing the train derail once again, perhaps permanently.

It's hard to understand why some people would think that way, but the world is full of a variety of people with differing mindsets.

The inner child in me, hopes that those viewing with the glass half empty,

will one day see the beauty of that glorious fire red engine train, including the faded paint chips.

The good news is, that the Choo Choo train has thousands of mileage left and many destinations yet to be seen.

Dark Cocoon

I am alive, but not living.

I am awake, but not awakened.

A cocoon is what I am.

Aware of life around me but not an active participant.

My existence is but a shell of who I really am.

My smile, laughter and cheerfulness are but a mask.

A mask which conceals my numbness.

If numbness was a sound, it would be a deafening sound.

How I wish to stop the deafening sound.

How I wish to break the binding membranes of this cocoon.

How I wish to shatter this deceiving mask.

How I wish to scream out loud in pain.

My wish is to breathe in a rhythmic manner and truly be alive.

To be freed from a numb existence, from this dream state.

I want again to be part of this amazing world.

To walk and rejoice amongst the living.

I want to live and be alive.

Second Chance At Living

How wonderful it is to have a second chance at life.

The opportunity to live a "normal" functioning day to day life.

I'll strike the quote unquote with the term normal.

Normal is what I want.

The opportunity presents itself, yet your mind convinces you to negate that opportunity.

One genuinely wants to grab the Bull by its horns, how close yet unreachable.

The mind is so complex and difficult to control.

Instead of your mind allowing you to have that second chance, it tells you, stay within the comfort of the four walls of your home and your mind.

That inner thought tells you, stay home, I will take care of you and comfort you.

No need to grasp that opportunity in living life. Your comfort is at home.

No need for social contact, no need to be embraced by the real world.

I ask my mind to set me free.

Free of darkness.

Free of fear.

Free of the chains that bound me to the comfort of my home.

Free to allow me to integrate back into the beautiful world I know exists.

Yes, I belonged to that wonderful world and environment at one time.

Yet, I allowed the dark and irrational thoughts of my mind to imprison me entirely.

Embrace me in a manner where it has become uncontrollable, unable to set myself free.

Yet, there are those moments, where I know I will be in touch with the beautiful world and all that encompasses it.

Yes, one must make an effort to break the chains and let go of fear and insecurity.

I have faith that his will happen.

I'm just waiting for that moment to escape these boundaries which falsely convinces me that I'm fine.

The convincing illusion of these walls which falsely gives me comfort being bound to in a safe environment.

My hope and wish is to break down the walls, rid myself of this damaging illusion.

Soon, I will live a normal life.

I'm not sure when this will happen, but I will certainly work hard at reaching that goal.

The goal is genuine happiness.

Yes, happiness, no more darkness.

That is my wish.

It will take work, but I feel the freshening air from afar of the world which I want to belong to.

It is palpable, not reachable yet.

But soon, I will grab the bulls by the horns and live freely.

Free to live life as should be.

Fleeting Anger

At this moment, anger has set in and is burning like a bed of coals.

I can't comprehend this negative emotion, but it is overwhelming.

I don't know if the anger is towards myself or directed to the world.

The anger of not being where I know I should and could be.

The anger of not being in control of my life.

I know this is a temporary and fleeting feeling and it too shall pass.

For me, not fast enough.

Although an irrational thought, Death would be welcome.

I shall conquer this, but at this time, I will allow it to flow through me.

It's a normal emotion, but I never invited it to my life.

Mind overflowing with thoughts.

The need to be in control.

Let this not allow me to become jaded in life.

I want to feel and project love and peace.

This feeling does not personify me.

Lord and Universe, let this pass, inundate me with peace and clarity of mind.

Gratefulness

Thank you, God.

Thank you, Universe.

You are One and the same.

I am fortunate to have so many wonderful people by my side.

A wonderful family and good friends.

I thank you Universe for bringing and blessing me with these special beings in my life.

I can share my joy and laughter with them.

I can share my sadness and tears with them.

I can celebrate my triumphs with them and feel their content in seeing my happiness.

Their support for me is so evident when it is truly needed.

I thank you, for their existence in my life is much needed, treasured and so much appreciated.

Thank you for this blessing bestowed upon me.

Darkness Descends

Oh My God!

Darkness has descended once again.

Just when Light was palpable and at arm's length,

It has quickly disappeared, the light no longer seen.

I ponder whether the light was there at all.

 Whether it was only my mind using a defense mechanism to get me through moments of desperation.

The grand, tall beautiful trees and flowers which gave me comfort and hope in the morning,

Is slowly leaving my view.

The comfort is dwindling away.

Darkness is overwhelming me once more, robbing me of the hope of living a healthy life and erasing the smile from my face.

I'm becoming a shell of what I once was.

I may be losing my mind.

How I yearn to have that light back into my life, whether real or an illusion, I would accept it with open arms.

Nonetheless, I will continue to battle this evil darkness.

I wonder if this darkness is self-imposed, a brain chemical imbalance or just a trial I must live with.

I look into the mirror and although I smile, beyond that smile is despair.

I know this darkness has a name.

It is named depression, deep depression.

God, I need your intervention.

Please send a ray of light my way, to give me hope that I will heal.

Hi Daddy

Although the day commenced with darkness,

An unexpected beautiful blessing materialized.

Thank you, Daddy.

It's been several years since you left my side,

I prayed from deep in my heart for you to stay, but God had a different plan.

With time I conformed and resigned to the reality of my loss.

There were many years where we could not relate as Father and Son.

Beyond our control, perhaps mine.

I did not feel the love and relationship I needed.

Eventually I faced it and although difficult, I accepted the relationship as it was.

Although unspoken, I perceived that you believed I was not the perfect son.

Not to your liking.

I do not apologize for being me.

The best that I could be, with faults and virtues.

I hope you finally realized that, and I believe you finally accepted me as I am.

That is what I have wished.

With all that said, I always loved you and I'm sure you loved me in your own way and I thank you.

Today, I raised my arms to the sky and unexpectedly,

I felt your presence near me during this dark moment.

I felt your support and love.

This feeling of love is what I always yearned.

You fulfilled my being with that love and acceptance and I thank you.

I easily perceived you standing by my side.

It seemed so "normal".

I was not astonished nor afraid.

I immediately, said "Hi Daddy!"

At this time, I cannot recall with absolute certainty, if I greeted you vocally or expressed it within my mind.

I knew you were there to support me and you communicated that all will be ok.

I will always remember this experience and I thank you once again.

I love you Daddy.

Deep Darkness Of Sleep

That deep dark moment of sleep is inevitable.

The time for that sleep cannot be predicted, but we know sooner or later, we will all experience it.

A sleep from which we will never awaken.

Many times, I wish for that dark peaceful sleep to manifest when I lay in my bed.

The dark sleep will mean no more pain.

The dark sleep will bring peace to my body, mind and soul.

No more worries or painful thoughts.

Yes, morbid desires and thoughts, but very real.

Yet I realize, I still have goals I want to attain in Life.

I realize I have responsibilities to take care of before that moment ever arrives.

Once I am confident that I have taken care of all loves ones and met my life's responsibilities,

Funny, as if I have a say, I will allow that dark deep moment of sleep to take over.

No need to grieve my absence in this mundane existence.

I ask that you rejoice and wish me well in my ultimate moment of peace.

If at all possible, I will watch over all my beautiful loved ones from where I ever exist in spirit.

Ah, one day, that moment of that dark peaceful sleep will arrive.

It will happen on the right day or night, at the appropriate time and place.

I await and welcome that peace.

2016.

My Wish

My deepest and sincerest wish is for you to be happy.

You have been through many trials, yet have accomplished great things.

Focus on those accomplishments.

Focus on wonderful memories.

You are a blessing from God and have touched many.

You have touched many in ways you may not be aware of, but know now that you have.

Now is the time for you, your happiness.

Know that you are deserving of what we all strive for, happiness.

It is your turn, welcome it.

This does not mean that you will neglect all the great things you have done, this will only magnify your kindness and generosity towards others.

Do not deny yourself, embrace happiness.

All will rejoice when they see that smile.

Once you embrace this deserving gift, you will radiate this beauty into your world, it will be contagious.

You will project happiness inwardly and outwardly.

If you only knew how this will affect all people you come in touch with.

Hold close this blessing meant for all.

My wish is for you to be happy.

Scream

At times we suppress our deep emotions, natural or not so natural thoughts and actions.

Perhaps because they are frightening to face, therefore we inhibit that which we perceive as unnatural.

While smiling in the mirror all seems fine, suddenly the urge to scream manifests.

One invokes all strength and will, inhibiting that deep crying sound from being audible.

If it was to be heard, it would make the hairs stand up on end on anyone near or far.

One holds it in and pray, that the sound does not reach the top of one's voice, that the mouth does not open and declare to the world the frightening despair, hopelessness and darkness in one's soul that is well locked within oneself.

At that very moment, one is perplexed as why this moment of despair transpired.

Accumulated painful experiences which have reached a peak, a volcano that has withheld eruption for a long time that can no longer contain its lava.

A lava that wants to overflow and let its presence be seen by all.

Lord, Universe, let this not happen again.

Most of all, if it does, may the scream be not audible to anyone but oneself.

Let it be muffled in a small space.

Otherwise, one will be labeled insane.

Not fit for society.

Judged by all.

Out of control.

Let this not happen again.

May that overwhelming feeling to scream disappear.

The Healing Of The Divine

Oh, my beautiful Divine,

I praise you in all your known names.

I acknowledge your presence and divine power in my life.

Although at times, despair sets in, your healing and beautiful light become only a blur of your power,

I know YOU are comforting and consoling me during arduous times.

Life will not always be a bed of roses, I will have to deal with the thorns and admire the beauty of your creation on Earth.

My faith is so strong, that I know I will overcome all difficulties and trials that are set before me in my paths.

Many know you by different names; God, Jesus Christ, Allah, Olodumare, Olofi, Krishna, Buddha and the many representations and avatars as Angels, Saints and Martyrs.

To me, You are One and the Same.

I ask you to look at me with your eternal love and merciful eyes and bring me good health, good fortune, prosperity and abundance.

I ask you to bring divine healing to my body, mind and soul.

I open my body, mind and soul to receive your divine energy.

Let this beautiful divine energy penetrate every cell of my body and mind.

Let this energy dissolve all illness from my body.

My body and mind may be broken now, but I know this is only temporary.

I believe divine healing is palpable, close and real.

Inundate me with this divine energy, destroy all malignancies and illness from my body and replace it with only positive and healthy cells.

I believe in you, my heart is yours.

I ask that divine healing, be realized at this very moment.

Your healing will allow me to love you even more, if that is even possible as my love for you is infinite.

This will allow me to praise you in all your manifestations and continue my work within spiritual paths you have assigned to me.

Heal me, heal me, heal me now.

There is nothing impossible for You.

That is my demonstration of faith and love for you.

May I have many years to continue my spiritual path and help others as you have always helped me.

I thank you now and always as I know my fervent wish for divine healing will be realized now.

The Unwelcome Visitor

As I shaved my face carefully and looked in the mirror,

I could sense that an unwelcome presence in my life would visit again.

Continuing to wash my face, I felt the dread, the fear.

The tears started to flow down my cheeks.

Washing off the tears and trying to maintain composure.

I covered my mouth to drown out my sobs.

I covered my mouth to cover the uncontrollable scream as to not alarm others.

Although muffled by my hands, the sound of the scream managed to come out.

In the privacy of my room, I drank coffee and cried.

During my prayers, as much as I tried to be calm, I cried.

On my way to go outside, I opened the door.

The unwelcome visitor was there to envelope my mind and soul.

I cried.

Breathing fresh air would do me well, so I thought.

The fresh air, breeze and bright sun, did nothing to alleviate the sadness and desperation that settled in.

I cried and wiped my eyes.

I cried and wiped my eyes.

I cried and wiped my eyes.

Arriving back home was a relief.

No need to hide the emotions.

I cried.

The unwelcome visitor is relentless.

His grip on my being is tight like a vice.

The wave of darkness flowed over me.

I accept it at this time, I do not have the strength to fight him off.

Not yet.

I will allow his presence to stay with me a while longer.

I will not pressure myself to fight when the strength is not within me.

I shall sleep.

Tomorrow is another day.

Thank You

Thank you, my most Glorious and Merciful Lord!

I have awakened this day full of life once again, thanks to you!

Each day that I wake up allows me to praise your heavenly name.

I shall praise your name and not just through words, but through my daily works and actions.

That is the least that I can do for all the wonderful blessings you have and continue to bestow upon me.

I praise you Lord, in all of your manifestations and names that are representative of you.

Though your names and manifestations may differ to some, through your divine enlightenment You are One to me.

I thank and praise you.

Unsustainable Anger

At this very moment in time,

The anger within is unsustainable.

Overwhelming.

Angry that I'm unable to help the person that I most love.

A feeling of helplessness.

An unfathomable and incomprehensible affliction.

Angry that the Universe has been unfair.

Angry with the unexpected, the unforeseen.

Angry that I feel alone.

Angry that my faith is faltering.

My faith is such a strong part of my life.

Let my faith not falter, weaken in the face of this trial.

Oh Lord, help in strengthening my faith in You and the Good that the Universe has to offer.

Do not allow me to fall into a dark abyss as I may not be able to lift myself up.

Strength, faith and acceptance is what I need.

Allow my faith and love to flourish once more.

I need it at this very moment and the future to come.

Anger is not the emotion that defines me.

May this anger subside and be replaced with peace.

Lord and Magnificent Universe, I ask that you be merciful and envelop my most loved one with a balm of complete healing, calm and peace.

The Lighthouse

Thank you Lord and Universe,

For the gift of allowing me the first thing to see, The Lighthouse.

Born from the darkness, I see the light emanating from The Lighthouse.

Allowing me to see all that surrounds my being.

Throughout my life that Lighthouse has always been ingrained my mind, both consciously and subconsciously.

Do Light Lighthouses have names?

There have been times where the skies were a brilliant blue and I was unable to perceive that beauty.

Yet I could not perceive that beauty due to darkness which was disillusioning and did not allow me to see that light.

At the most appropriate time, the bright warm beams of warm light emanating from the Lighthouse inundated my sight and mind and allowed me to see that beauty which I could not feel or perceive.

This Lighthouse has been my rock and will always be for all time.

All through the storms we all experience, the Lighthouse has been my savior.

Disallowing me to wallow in desperation, the light guiding me to the surface of humanity and the beautiful surroundings inhabiting what we call Earth.

The Lighthouse has always been vigilant, watching my every move, illuminating my every step.

At times during my life, I ignored the light and walked into dark alley ways.

The Lighthouse never gave up on me.

The emanating light pierced all walls of darkness to prove to me that she will always be there, never allowing me to be lost.

I instinctively know that this beautiful Lighthouse, battered by storms, the Sun and all elements will not always be in my life.

The years have taken its toll and at a given time will not be spiritually or physically near me.

The great miracle is, that this Lighthouse will forever be engrained in my mind, has taught me lessons and given me warmth and that shall never be forgotten.

I will look to these memories in times of strife and difficult periods as well as remember this light in wonderful times in my life.

Yes! Yes! Yes!

I couldn't remember the name of this Lighthouse but was always there in my heart and mind.

The Lighthouse is named Mother.

Thank you, Mother, my Lighthouse, for always being that beaming light of hope, life and faith in my life!

The Year 2016

The smile on his face barely disguises that lack of luster of life in his eyes.

He is tired and only wishes to sleep for a full day.

Unfortunately, his daily responsibilities do not allow that luxury.

He continues to fight the fatigue, the tiredness, the desperation with a smile on his face.

The smile is a strategy, a deterrent to have his observers focus on the smile instead of his eyes.

2016.

Although he fights with all his might, he is tired.

Physically tired.

Mentally tired.

Spiritually tired.

Desperation.

2016.

He continues to make others smile as if on a last mission.

Leaving happiness and joy with those he encounters.

His wish is to inspire and heal others in many aspects.

2016.

Yes, the last mission.

Truly affect others with words of encouragement and inspiration,

Although he feels none in his deepest part of his soul.

He grasps and grasps, but that happiness, that healing is not existent, not reachable.

2016.

He believes 2016 is his last chance to leave a legacy behind before he departs the earthly plane.

He continues to smile until the smile is frozen on his face.

2016.

Darkness.

No more tiredness or fatigue.

No more fear.

No more desperation.

His hope has been that he completed his mission.

2016.

Sandman's Visit

As I usually do at night,

I tucked my beautiful girl into bed.

Covered her with her favorite blanket and kissed her affectionately on her forehead,

Wishing her a good night.

It's been several nights where she has not had a good night's sleep.

My hope at that very moment, was for her to rest peacefully and have picturesque candy dreams.

Shortly thereafter, I went to bed to rest and wish for a peaceful sleep.

Mr. Sandman came to mind.

Sandman.

I dozed off for a few minutes, only to wake up and think of my child's sleep.

I couldn't contain myself.

I decided to tip toe to her room and take a look.

It was such a delightful sight.

Sandman was so kind to visit her as she laid in her bed.

I could see a lovely tear on her left eye in the shape of a diamond.

She was fast asleep and a smile on her face.

Dreaming with angels.

She slept throughout the night without interruption.

She awoke with such an upbeat attitude.

Brushed her teeth and combed her lovely shiny hair.

At the breakfast table, she told me she had a serene magical night which encompassed colorful sweet dreams.

Sandman, thank you for visiting my child and making her happy.

Let it not be your last visit.

Remember

Before I forget,

I must write.

Feverishly write, to all,

to all whom I have met, liked and loved.

Before I forget, I share and write my thoughts, perhaps real or unreal fears.

Dammit, I will not fool you.

I will not sugarcoat.

These are my fears.

Please, remember me from then and not from the now.

Remember my sense of humor.

Remember my love of Life, my love of God, of seeing the good in others.

Remember my love and respect for all paths of spirituality.

Remember that I strived to be a better person in life.

Remember my dislike of injustice.

Remember my joy of dancing.

Remember my excitement of learning.

Remember my joy of teaching.

Remember my joy of mentoring friends and colleagues.

Remember my compassion.

Remember my love of helping others as much as I could, which brought me so much satisfaction.

Remember my joy of writing.

Remember me from then and not from the now.

Remember my zaniness.

Remember my laughter.

Remember my smile.

Remember my hugs and affection.

Remember my hello kisses.

Remember me from then and not from the now.

Remember me for the embracing the joy of all types of festivities.

Halloween, Birthdays, Christmas and Mother's Day.

Remember me for the love of family and friends.

Oh yes, how I can forget.

My faults are part of these memories, remember them as all.

My sense of humor is still intact, therefore, try not to focus on my faults.

Do forgive me if I ever offended you.

Remember.

I feverishly write as to not forget.

When my smile is no longer there and just a frozen line.

Remember.

When my words are no longer audible.

Remember.

When I'm unable to recall your name.

Remember.

When my memories are faulty.

Remember.

If I become difficult and feisty.

Remember.

I feverishly write to remember.

I love you.

Always remember.

I feverishly write and scream out,

Please, remember me from then and not from the now.

Remember.

Promise me that you will remember.

Beloved Ancestors

My beloved Ancestors, my family members residing in Heaven.

I pay homage to you.

To those who came before me and after me who are no longer in this corporal world of existence.

I pay homage and respect.

To those whose blood courses through the veins of my parents and mine, I acknowledge your most important existence in my life.

I ask that you share the wisdom you acquired here on earth with me.

Now that you are in the spiritual realm of truth, I ask that you share that divine wisdom with me.

Impart that great wisdom onto me so that I can live life with good character.

Enlighten me so that I can make correct decisions in life.

Should I close my ears to your guidance out of ignorance, enlighten me once more.

May I learn from my mistakes, set my feet firmly on the ground and sprint forward with the acquired wisdom.

I ask that you steer away those that may not have the best of intentions for me.

I ask that you lift my spirits when my faith is frail.

Inspire me always to keep close contact with you.

Keep my eyes, ears and mind clear so I can always perceive, receive and interpret any advice and messages you have for me.

May each day I get to form a closer bond with you.

Thank you for the infinite wisdom you lovingly share with me.

Thank you for your presence in my life.

One day as the sages say, we will be one, flowing together; our blood will be as in the beginning of time.

Accepting Accountability

Accept accountability for the situations that you are presently living.

The easy path which may be relieving to your mind, is to blame others or blame God, The Divine, and The Universe in all its beautiful manifestations.

No.

Take a moment to sit down and analyze your life, your past behaviors and actions towards others and yourself, and you will find the reason of being to your current situation.

In many major religions and spiritual paths, there is a term called Karma.

The definition of this term is cause and effect.

What you have done, good or bad, will have an outlying outcome in your present or future.

The aforementioned is similar if not the same as the Christian and Judaic phrase of "You reap what you sow" in Holy Scriptures.

Have you treated your parents with love and respect?

If not, very likely, you will live through what your parents experienced.

On the other hand, you may be fortunate, your children will treat you well and this will allow you to contemplate on your past actions.

How have you treated your friends and family?

How have they treated you?

If there were transgressions, have you allowed rancor to settle into your heart or have you forgiven?

Think about it and therein lies the solution or response.

How successful are you in your career or in school?

Did you strive to study and go above and beyond to excel? Sincerely responding to that question will give provide insight.

It is never too late to correct or improve your situation.

At times, our living situations or social status may be difficult.

Through your strong will, determination and unwavering faith in the Divine is key.

Yes, the struggle can be real, but you can overcome it.

Although harsh to express, at times we blame the Divine for our health issues.

We have been gifted with free will.

How have you treated your body as a young person?

Healthy diet?

Did you indulge in excessive drinking, smoking or other unhealthy habits?

Very likely, your answer lies there.

No.

We cannot blame the Divine for the choices we have made during our lifetime.

There are some that follow the school of thought, that we have lived life more than once, in other past existences.

Within there lies, the belief of Karma within Buddhism and Hinduism and other spiritual paths.

Perhaps in those past lives, we weren't the best that we could be.

Consequently, our souls are born again through reincarnation, and we must start all over or suffer the pains we caused others in those past lives.

At times, we "reap" what our ancestors "sowed".

Now that is a hard pill to swallow.

We should try to understand, if not, accept what our ancestors did and remedy, correct their past actions.

We also live or witness situations that are truly unfathomable in the world and lives of others.

At times, unexplainable.

We seek understanding as to why, yet that insight is not provided.

If you live a spiritual or religious life, the answer may be present.

Many times, we will say that it is the will of the Divine.

Perhaps in the future we will learn the "why".

Let's contemplate.

Look deeply within your mind and soul, and the reason of your current situation may be revealed.

Perhaps not entirely at once.

Give it time.

Personally, I've had troublesome times in my life.

I am not perfect.

That being said, I accept responsibility for any past transgressions, literally and figuratively.

Then, I try my best to take action to rectify and to remedy my current situation.

Acknowledging and accepting self-responsibility is not always easy, but it is certainly a step forward to a better life and future.

Truth and wisdom is distributed amongst all.

Ask And You Shall Receive

My Lord, in the sacred scriptures you state, "Ask and ye shall receive".

I humbly come to you and this moment and ask for your assistance.

I find myself in a struggling battle which I have to conquer.

These dark, cold walls of steel surround me of which appears no escape.

Though I pound my fists on these walls with all my strength, they are unrelenting.

I feel like I am imprisoned in a deep and dark abyss.

This darkness envelopes me with desperation, anxiety, loneliness, depression and lack of hope.

Deep inside I know this battle is to pass, that there is a light of salvation in the not too far distance.

I ask that you fill my heart and mind with the light of hope.

Fortify my faith.

Lift my spirit high to the heavens and allow me to see that the battle will soon be over and things will be alright.

I know that with your help I will be whole again.

Your divine light will make me whole and I will rejoice.

I will once more praise your name and works.

Come, hurry!

Make me once again the child of hope, happiness and joy that you created.

Thank you, for I know in asking I shall receive.

Hear My Plea

My Dear Lord,

I humbly kneel at your feet and bow my head before you.

I ask that you hear my plea.

I ask that you cast your merciful eyes upon this living being which was divinely created by you.

My heart overflows with sorrow and sadness to see this brethren suffer with this affliction.

Please overlook any flaws and imperfections that he may project.

His virtues, good heart and good intentions I am confident will outweigh all flaws.

I ask that you lay your miraculous hands upon his body.

Heal and make him whole again.

Remove the pain and suffering from his body.

Allow your divine benevolent energy to enter and penetrate every living cell in his body.

That this wonderful energy dissolves all disease and illness.

Make his body whole and new again as before.

Your Power over spirit and matter is absolute.

Your will be done.

Your name is praised for your merciful and miraculous works.

Like That Man

That clean cut youthful man,

Projecting a refreshing outlook on life.

His daily business attire, crisp blue, white, pink shirts with clean sharp creases displayed from shoulder to wrist.

Adventurous as well with bright colored shirts emitting joie de vivre.

Dressed on weekends comfortably with snug jeans, relaxed t-shirts.

Casual footwear with beautiful colorful shoe laces.

The overall wardrobe reflecting his true inner self, cheerfulness.

Walking with a shining smile, confidence to conquer the world,

On his merry way, greeting both strangers and friends alike with "Good morning!"

A joy for life that he exudes, living for life.

The glass half full, even overflowing.

Ah, yes.

That was me not to long ago in my past.

His sincere outlook to life was mine as well.

Not very long ago, I projected the same joy for life.

The confidence to bring joy to others and myself.

That dimmed, not too very long ago.

If I take a moment to take a deep look into my being,

That light hidden within the depths of my soul.

Dimmed, but the flame of light is still there, barely lit.

I have hope that light, that flame of life, will reignite in all its glory.

Yes, once again, that light will shine from within to the world.

It may take time, but it will reappear.

I will revive the same outlook as that beautiful young man.

The passion for life.

The compassion for those around me.

The contagious smile and laughter.

Yes.

I will once again, be me.

Me.

May it be soon, very soon.

I Forgive You

As difficult as this action is for many of us,

I forgive you.

Whether your hurtful words and actions were intentional or not,

I forgive you.

My heart does not have room for rancor.

My mind does not have room for jadedness.

No room for cynicism.

I am naturally that way.

No claims to sainthood, holding grudges and enduring piercing thorns have never defined me as a person.

As I cleanse myself of hurt emotions, I forgive you.

I wish you peace.

I wish you enlightenment to not hurt others,

To measure your words and actions.

I in turn, ask all, to forgive me if I have offended anyone in anyway.

Life is short, we do not know what tomorrow holds.

I clear my heart and mind of transgressions towards me.

May you understand and accept me as I am one day.

Forgiveness brings me relief in a way you may not understand.

I am at peace.

I wish you peace, tranquility and love in your life.

I forgive you.

The Divine is grand.

I am confident the Divine will understand and forgive you as well.

The Unspoken Of Sanctuary

A place where we seek and find comfort.

A place where we can express ourselves without inhibitions.

The bathroom shower?

Yes, it can be a sanctuary for some but not mentioned to others in our daily lives.

A place for physical refinement.

A place for silence, exhilaration and spiritual cleansing as well.

Where our singing sounds great to our ears, perfect timbre.

Where we bow our heads to feel the comforting mix of cold and hot water to massage the back of our necks.

Where we wash our hair and scalp and find the sensation exhilarating.

Where we using a foaming soap to clean every pore of our body, what a beautiful feeling.

Where we can stay in the shower as long as we want, no rush, our secret sanctuary.

Where we can pray without interruption and praise God in all his manifestations for another day of life and blessings.

We may decide not to confide this invigorating experience to others, but it's undoubtedly there for our daily escape and comfort.

It's ok to keep this to ourselves.

Our secret of a restorative moment.

Sense Of Hopelessness

As he carefully looks into the mirror, there is no doubt that he is not what he was a short time ago.

Definitely not the commissioned painting initially requested by Dorian Gray.

The healthy and vibrant look of life has diminished rapidly, in a blink of an eye.

The full rosy cheeks replaced by that sunken appearance of illness, sockets.

The body that was once toned is now loose skin hanging on to the skeletal bones of the body.

His ribs are visible.

His spinal cord is visible.

His pectoral muscles are miniscule.

The body in total appears fragile and weak.

His eyes are not vibrant but opaque.

The frightening part of his current assessment of his body is, whether good health will reappear once again.

He has no desire for others to see him in this condition, creating a defeating complex.

His deepest desire is to be healthy again, yet at times he feels there may be no help to uplift his very being.

That is his state of mind.

A sense of hopelessness.

His desire to remove this complex is present, but not easy to overcome.

He has a sense of hope, although distant.

Ah, hope is hard to grasp and at arm's length.

How Are You?

How are you?

A formal yet straightforward question we ask others we encounter on a daily basis.

It is part of the etiquette our parents taught us.

The response of "fine, thank you" or acknowledgement of your greeting with a nod is generally expected.

At times, we expect a more personable response, inquiring the same of you.

As a friend once mentioned in the past, it's "just a formality" which I found odd.

During this summer's early evening, it was raining and overcast.

I dashed out of my apartment to throw out the garbage in the door enclosed garbage chute.

I decided that I would take a quick look at the small garden in the building's courtyard.

I love flowers, a reminder of life.

On my way, I unexpectedly ran into a neighbor.

I was not ready for this encounter.

Evidently, returning from a summer stroll with her beautiful child in one hand and the baby stroller in her other.

Of course, I greeted her with "How are you?".

She responded with "I'm fine, thank you. How are you?"

I smiled and said "I'm fine, thank you."

It was a very quick greeting.

The encounter was paralyzing.

Instead of taking a few steps to see the garden,

I quickly turned around with tear filled eyes to avoid another unexpected encounter.

I returned to my apartment and securely locked my door.

Uncontrollably, the tears flowed.

I did not respond honestly.

Fine I was not. Not then, not now.

Her polite response and question hit home.

The encounter which took less than a few minutes, reminded me that I am not fine.

Most people expect a simple formality to be short lived.

It was not for me.

Exposing your personal reality in that moment is not expected by your counterpart.

Most are not prepared to hear "I'm not fine" and respond with empathy or respond at all.

Their mind, due to life experience is wired to hear that all is well and may not capture the "not".

If they are close friends or family members, perhaps the "not" is heard.

How are you?

Reality Or Imagination

Thank you for treating me to the wonderful brunch at the quaint café.

I enjoyed the dark aromatic espresso freshly brewed from the Colombian coffee beans.

Topping it off was the scrumptious mouthwatering blueberry scone.

Such a delight to my inviting taste buds.

The conversation was a complement to our light meal.

I couldn't ask for more.

Thank you.

It begs the question whether this experience was real.

Although this experience was so vivid, the uncertainty remains, whether this was a dream or a figment of my imagination.

The fine line between reality and lunacy.

How I wish this pleasant encounter was real.

Perhaps it was, perhaps it wasn't.

Was this a dream or reality?

My mind is possibly deceiving me.

Challenging me to decipher between reality and illusion.

My hope is that my mind is clear and calm to interpret this experience and solve the truth.

The mind is so complex.

Divine Saint Michael

Oh Glorious and Divine, Saint Michael.

I respectfully salute and greet you.

I invoke your mighty presence in my life.

Most beautiful yet humble Archangel,

I call you.

He who is Captain of the Legion of Angels that guard over the heavenly realm, I call you.

He who declared war against those that rose up against our Father in heaven and won victoriously, I call you.

Most wonderful Saint Michael, Archangel, Protector against evil,

I ask that you be forever present in my life and of those that I love.

I ask that you envelope and protect my being and those that I love with your immense wings in times of danger.

That you guide me and mine to a secure place filled with peace and love until the storm is over.

In the days filled with hate and terrorism, protect me and mine.

May we always find solace in you and each other.

May we never get lost in this world that is full of light but where darkness may at times descend.

Protect us from the malevolent actions of those with darkened souls.

May their deeds and ill will never touch us.

Fend off any evil projected toward us with your mighty and indestructible sword.

Enlighten us to keep out of evil's way.

Guide us into the righteous path in life.

I surrender my being and those of whom I love into your hands.

Protect us always while asleep or awake.

As I pray all this to you, it is realized.

Thank you most Glorious One.

I ask for all in the name of our Heavenly Father and Jesus Christ.

Breaking Free From The Dark Web

There are times when a dark menacing web unexpectedly appears out of the shadows without warning.

It envelopes your very being, mind and soul.

The fibers which appear to be constructed of black silk fiber is strong as any metal made.

It wraps around you tightly, the fear settles in that you will not be able to break these fibers and will remain trapped in this web.

Unwittingly, you see a speck of light that penetrates the web, which you thought would never see.

That light gives you hope and strength.

Eventually that strength makes you realize, that the fiber is not made of iron, the metal was just an illusion.

You begin to strike with the innate strength you were born with at that web to break free from that darkness.

The dark web disappears into nothingness, a void never to be felt or seen.

Realization sets in that you are much stronger than that darkness and are surrounded, filled by a light of love and faith.

The light was always within you, just dimmed.

You are free.

From that moment on, you will not allow that dark web to deceive you, as the light will always be within to break it.

Is The Light Real?

After being inundated in so much darkness for what seemed infinity, the light is so very welcome.

The light represents joy and happiness which seemed so elusive a day ago.

Naturally, I am questioning this light.

Why has it appeared after spending so much time chasing it?

So much time, praying and pleading for it to reenter my life of darkness.

I question the sudden appearance of this light.

Will its presence with me be just temporary?

Is it here just to provide relief for my mind to remain intact?

A divine protection to help my mind for a moment, to avoid an inevitable madness?

Perhaps an illusion created by an overwhelmed mind?

I pray that it will not be so.

That it's not an illusion created by a powerful and tricky mind.

Let this light be infinite.

Let the happiness and joy be a reality that will not escape or abandon me.

Only time will tell, if I'm living and experiencing this moment of light.

I will learn from each passing day when I awake each morning, whether this light is real or artificial.

My hope is that that is an unending reality.

I pray and hope this is not a cruel joke of the Universe to prolong an unending and overwhelming torment.

My Sweet Jesus

My Sweet Jesus.

Lord and Savior of the World.

My Teacher.

My Friend.

I ask that you come into my life and fulfill me.

I ask that you bring calmness to my mind so that I can sense your presence by my side.

I ask that you fill my heart with peace and love so that it mirrors the compassion of your sacred heart.

I ask that you replace any loneliness with your loyal companionship.

That I may feel your consoling warm hands on my shoulder when I am feeling sad or down.

That I may feel your fraternal cheerfulness and joy when I celebrate great moments in life.

That I may always celebrate life in your Spirit.

I know that I shall receive, thank you!

Life

Ah, Life.

The Gift of Life.

Life is beautiful, it truly is a gift like no other.

A gift we should embrace.

For many of us that are fortunate, it is a long school of learning and experiences.

Some good, some not as good.

Yes, it will show and teach us many amazing things throughout our existence here on earth.

This brings about maturity.

If we are perceptive and open to learning, we will not reencounter obstacles that were present in the past.

As wonderful as Life is, we will also experience moments of trials, sadness, desperation and loss.

This is inevitable.

This is the law of the Universe.

There has to be a balance in order for us to appreciate Life.

We will encounter very dark moments where our anguish will not allow us to see beyond the darkness, where the hope of light does not seem within arm's reach.

Yet, at the very right time, this period will be replaced by a warm and healing Light.

That Light will embrace your existence and you will look back, and know that perhaps it was a lesson or experience you had to endure.

Enjoy and clasp every moment of Life.

Do not allow hopelessness to overcome you.

Life is unpredictable.

Your Life can reach a long or short span of time.

Enjoy it to the fullest.

Remove the thorns, resentfulness, bitterness, rancor, jadedness from your heart and mind.

These thoughts and feelings are not constructive, and one must not waste a moment of time.

Life is precious.

Live Life as it was the last day on Earth.

Life is good.

Grant Me Peace

When the deep blue waters are turbulent,

Furious and appear to be black,

Grant me Peace.

When the crystalline blue waters flow smoothly are sweet to the taste,

Grant me Peace.

When the heavens are dark, cloudy, stormy and are threatening,

Grant me Peace.

When the sky is clear, bright and filled with heavenly light,

Grant me Peace.

When darkness descends during the night and the air surrounding me is bitterly cold,

Grant me Peace.

When the shining rays of the Sun rise and radiate warmth awakening life,

Grant me Peace.

When I am in the presence of mankind with darkened souls projecting tribulation, sadness, depression and desperation,

Grant me Peace.

When people that are blessed with a great light in their souls and have enlightenment are put directly in my path,

Grant me Peace.

When illness of body, mind and spirit surround me,

Grant me Peace.

When abundant health, joy, happiness and love surround me,

Grant me Peace.

My Great and Wonderful Lord, grant me peace, everlasting peace in moments of lightness and darkness.

With Peace I will always be content.

Beloved Guardian Angels

My beloved Guardian Angels and Spirit Guides.

I acknowledge and recognize your presence in my life.

I am blessed that our Almighty God has handpicked you to guide me in this world.

Assist me in keeping and maintaining a clear mind.

Clarity of mind will allow me to better receive and interpret the advice and messages you have for me.

I open my heart, mind and soul to your divine wisdom and presence.

Though God has given all on Earth the gift of free will, I allow your will to be mine.

This which in turn is the will of our Great Lord.

Guide me to the paths that are correct and righteous.

Guide me to spiritual development and enlightenment.

Guide me to success in all my positive endeavors.

Guide me to a more enriched life.

Thank you, my beautiful beings of light, for your everlasting and infinite presence in my life.

The Rooster's Song

What energy and joie de vivre the morning rooster has upon the rising and expanding rays of the Sun!
The glorious song he so proudly sings, announcing the birth of a new day, is awakening to my ears and nourishing to my soul.
May that innate nature of the rooster blossom within me.
May that joy the rooster's song transmitted always resonate within me.
May the first words that I utter as I awaken in the morning are words of praise, praise to you!
As the rooster's song soothes my being, may the words that come from my mouth soothe and comfort those around me.
May my words and actions bring about joy and positive change to those that I meet and encounter.
May my being always be inundated with peace and blissfulness as it is when I hear the rooster's proud song.
Most of all, my dear Lord, that I always project this feeling of peace to all.

May they feel the transmission of this peace in their souls and mind.

Encased By White Debris

As I stand in the middle of the room,

I can hear the walls moving.

Slowly, but surely, trembling around me.

I stay still, without fear.

Knowing the outcome of what's to come.

The outside of the walls, starting to peel and crumble.

Once magnificent walls, falling apart.

I do not move, running away is not a desire.

My inner sense and instinct, allows me to stay.

As mounds of white washed wall start to fall,

I remain still.

Welcoming what is to come.

Mounds of wall start to accumulate around me.

Yet I remain still, no fear.

The white ceiling starts to peel, allowing the pressure from above to give in.

The dust slowly starts to cover my head and body.

My head and face is encased with debris.

The mounds of sheetrock, gently pound my body.

No fear.

The motion of it all becomes rapid.

I am totally covered from head to toe with the ceiling and surrounding walls.

Mummified.

No desire to escape from this at all.

Although covered with the heaviness of it, I can still breathe.

A slight pinhole, allows a bit of light to come in.

A sense of calm and peace overcomes me.

Most would want to claw and excavate to be released from this collapse.

Not me.

Strangely, this mummification brings me peace.

My desire is to remain encased.

Away from the world, recluse.

I do not seek rescue as it is not welcomed or desired.

Allow me to remain in this state of being, alone.

Do not seek me.

I feel peace from the outside world.

My hope is that no one heard the collapse.

No attempts to rescue what is left of me.

I am fine where I am.

Covered with debris.

I am at peace from the outside world.

No loneliness, inundated with peace and tranquility.

Sound and happy, from the surrounding collapse of wall and ceiling.

Serenity and stillness is finally here.

Yes, serenity.

Peace has inundated me, and I am fine.

Allow this to be, do not seek me out, I am well.

Made in United States
North Haven, CT
15 September 2024